A PICTURE OF HEALTH

Hospitals and Nursing on Old Picture Postcards

by

Cynthia O'Neill, S.R.N., S.C.M., Q.N., H.V.

Foreword by Trevor Clay, R.G.N., R.M.N., F.R.C.N.

S. B. Publications
1989

This book is dedicated to all my patients, many of whom are still alive today.

First published in 1989 by S. B. Publications.

5 Queen Margaret's Road, Loggerheads, Nr. Market Drayton, Shropshire, TF9 4EP.

ISBN 1 870708 23 7

Distributed in the U.K. by Macmillan Distribution Ltd., Houndmills Estate, Basingstoke, Hampshire, RG21 2XS.

Printed in Great Britain by Rubell Print Ltd., Bunbury, Tarporley, Cheshire, CW6 9PQ.

Bound by J W Braithwaite and Son Limited, Pountney Street, Wolverhampton WV2 4HY.

CONTENTS

ACKNOWLEDGEMENTS

The author wishes to thank the following people for their valuable assistance:

P. Viccars for the gift of the postcard on page 31
Alan Bower for the loan of the postcard on page 40
Dr. J. McCarthy for the loan of the postcard on page 48
P. Standley for the loan of the postcard on page 72
T. Allen for several military and naval postcards

The Most Rev. and Right Hon. Robert Runcie, Archbishop of Canterbury
The Archivist, Royal College of Nursing Library
The Queen's Nursing Institute
Bristol Public Library
Oxford Reference Library
Local History Research Group of Palmers Green Library
The Wellcome Museum of Medical Science
The Radcliffe Infirmary Archives and Photography Department
St. Joseph's Hospice, London
P. Strange
Christine Hoy
Dr. I. McLellan

Editorial: Gillian Jackson
Additional Editorial and Marketing: Steve Benz

Further Reading:
'A Beacon in our Town' by Christine Hoy
'British Hospital' by A. G. Ives
'Lectures in Surgical Nursing' by E. Stanmore Bishop, F.R.C.S.
'Nursing Lectures to Probationers' by S. Yapp
'District Nursing' by Mary Irven

FOREWORD

Cynthia O'Neill, herself a former nurse, has brought together, in this book, a collection of postcards which allows us a rare and fascinating glimpse of health care in the United Kingdom, in what we are so often asked to believe were "the good old days". Surely the nurses and other health care workers whom we see depicted here, would envy the "hi-tech" working environment which we, their modern counterparts, perhaps take for granted.

There is something here for everyone, whether collector or historian, patient or carer; an opportunity for an affectionate look back to how things used to be - and a graphic demonstration of the incredibly rapid progress achieved this century in so many areas of health care - although it has taken us nearly all this time to achieve the reforms in nursing education which we are convinced are necessary, in order to prepare nurses for their participation in tomorrow's health service.

Though some of the scenes captured in these postcards may appear to us to be stiff and formal, they clearly show real people in their contemporary environment and remind us that nurses and their colleagues have always worked within the constraints - whether social, technical or financial - of their own times, to serve their patients and clients to the best of their ability and knowledge.

Postcard collecting is becoming an increasingly popular hobby but this is more than a collection - in an original way it is a contribution to nursing history.

Trevor Clay, R.G.N., R.M.N., F.R.C.N.
April, 1989.

INTRODUCTION

Nursing really had no beginning but the growth of professional nursing, starting in 1854, came as a result of the working of the Poor Law, Florence Nightingale and the VAD movement. The Daughters of Charity of St. Vincent de Paul, in 1632 in France, were the first visiting or district nurses.

Nursing can never be regarded as a job - as Florence Nightingale said: "What is to be compared to dealing with the human body, The Temple of God's Spirit?"

Conditions in the Crimea were dreadful and it was Miss Nightingale, with her band of nurses and nuns, who improved matters. She was a woman of great administrative qualities and several of the English hospitals that she designed still proudly stand today. The public gave £40,000 to the Nightingale Fund, in gratitude for what had been done for the sick soldiers and, as a result, the Nightingale Training School for Nurses was opened at St. Thomas's Hospital, London, in July 1860, with fifteen probationers.

Advances in medical science and better nursing training raised the whole standard of patient care so that, by 1900, nursing had become an honoured and respectable profession for any young lady to enter. By 1919, there was State Registration. The College of Nursing was founded in 1916; it later became the Royal College of Nursing, which now has 284,000 members.

Nursing has never been an easy life - and it never will be. Neither will a nurse amass a fortune in the bank, but he or she will have a great store of happy memories to draw upon in later life.

Every patient has an identity. The 87-year-old, confused, bed-ridden and difficult at times, Mrs. Clarke was once a young girl and just as full of life as the nurse tending to her today.

Cynthia O'Neill.
22 Church Meadow,
Milton-under-Wychwood,
Near Oxford, OX7 6JG.
March, 1989.

WE ALL NEED NURSES

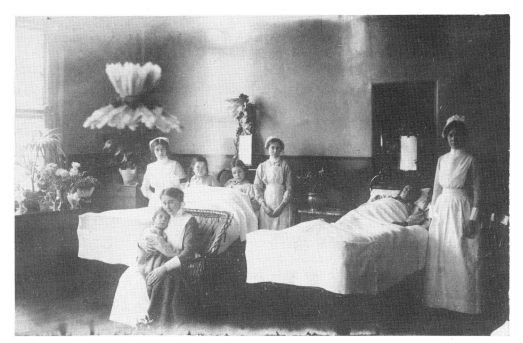

A WARD SCENE, UNKNOWN LOCATION, c. 1900
We all need nurses at some time in our lives. Nurses surround the mother and her baby and, throughout life, a nurse is often close at hand. The school nurse used to visit the school-children regularly, a service that is now, sadly, discontinued. Most large factories have a nurse ready to help when necessary. In this picture, notice the love that Sister is giving to the blind boy she is nursing and, in the bed behind, are they Siamese twins?

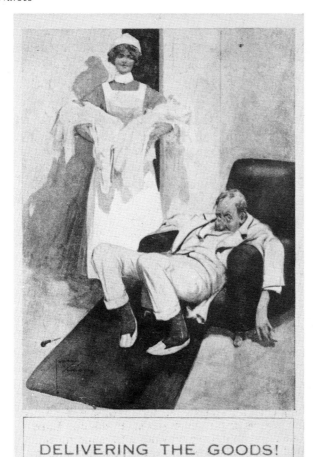

DELIVERING THE GOODS!

DELIVERING THE GOODS!
c. 1909
This example of Edwardian humour, showing the distressed father, was drawn by Lawson Wood. Long before a baby is born, it is the midwife who cares for the mother-to-be and her unborn baby, as he or she listens to its magical heartbeat. A midwife is usually a fully-trained nurse with additional midwifery training, so basically is a nurse and is often affectionately known as "The Nurse". Whether born at home or in hospital, each one of us has reason to be grateful to nurses.
(Published by Inter-Art Co.)

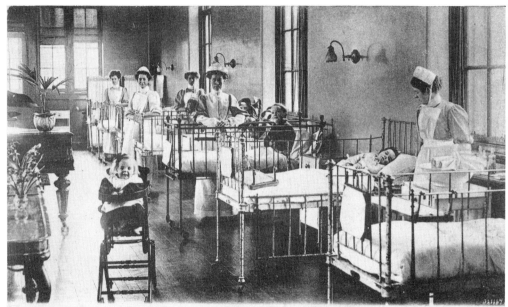

The Lady Caroline Charteris Ward of the Royal Hospital for Sick Children, Edinburgh.

LADY CAROLINE CHARTERIS WARD,
THE ROYAL HOSPITAL FOR SICK CHILDREN, EDINBURGH, c. 1906

The new baby soon grows up but, during childhood, may need admission to a children's ward. There was none of the free and easy visiting of today and many children hated hospitals. The piano in this ward would, no doubt, have provided a little merriment. Some hospitals had beautifully painted, tiled walls to occupy the little minds and, in some hospitals, one can see this tiling which is probably almost one hundred years old. Doctor Alexander Wood of Edinburgh gave the first injection of morphine using a syringe, in 1853.

THE CASUALTY, GENERAL HOSPITAL, CHELMSFORD, , c. 1905
During one's lifetime, few can escape a visit to the local casualty - now known as the A & E department. This casualty would have smelt strongly of "hospital". On the left of the picture, a gas fire provides heating and it looks as if the nurse is preparing a kaolin poultice. This was well before the age of antibiotics, so the only treatment for boils and nasty wounds was lancing and the application of soothing kaolin. Sister, in the dark dress and black belt, checks that the nurse has applied the bandage correctly.

VICTORIA WARD, RADCLIFFE INFIRMARY, OXFORD, c. 1908
Founded by Dr. John Radcliffe in 1770, this hospital still serves the city, university and
neighbouring towns and villages. The Victoria Ward is now used as a physiotherapy
department. A new hospital, known as J.R.11, stands on elevated ground overlooking the
old Infirmary.
(Photograph reproduced courtesy Oxfordshire County Council Libraries)

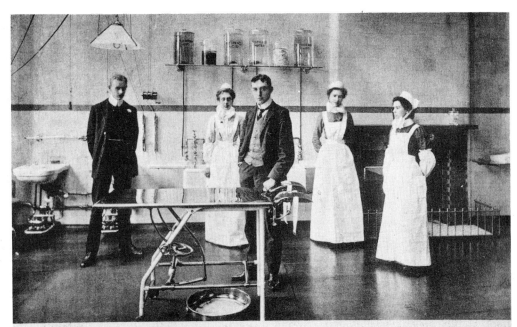

The Middlesex Hospital London W. *Prudhoe Operating Theatre*

PRUDHOE OPERATING THEATRE, THE MIDDLESEX HOSPITAL, c. 1910
For the operation, a chloroform mask would induce sleep while the surgeon used his skill. Students would climb the gallery steps to observe the great masters at work. Most patients dreaded an operation - but many lived to tell the tale. The Middlesex Hospital, in Mortimer Street, London, was founded in 1745 and rebuilt in 1929. Nurses at the hospital wore starched bows under their chins, which must have caused irritation. A fireplace, complete with fender and fireguard, warmed the cold, tiled room.

WARD 2, WOMAN'S HOSPITAL, BIRMINGHAM, c. 1909

This postcard is postmarked 4th March, 1909, and the message on the reverse reads: "Miss Thompson is going to have her operation tomorrow morning. She may have one visitor on Sunday for one hour. O. W. M. pro Sister". Miss Thompson could have had a hysterectomy under gas or ether and quite likely would have made a good recovery. Notice how the bed-legs are covered up - as was the custom in those days. This hospital continues to serve the women of Birmingham.

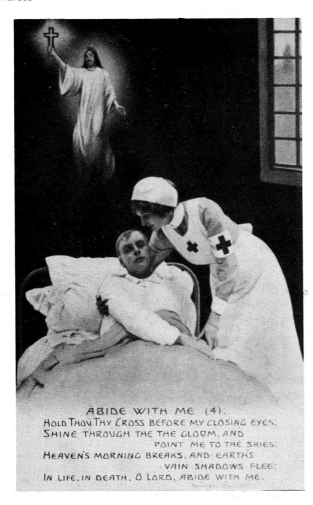

ABIDE WITH ME (4).
HOLD THOU THY CROSS BEFORE MY CLOSING EYES;
SHINE THROUGH THE THE GLOOM, AND
                    POINT ME TO THE SKIES;
HEAVEN'S MORNING BREAKS, AND EARTHS
                    VAIN SHADOWS FLEE;
IN LIFE, IN DEATH, O LORD, ABIDE WITH ME.

"ABIDE WITH ME", c. 1914
During World War 1, these cards were a very popular way of arousing patriotism and persuading VADs to volunteer. This is the final card of a set of four "song cards" illustrating this much-loved hymn. They were published by the famous firm of Bamforth & Co. Ltd.
The last honoured duty of any nurse is to tend his/her dying patient; the final duty being known as the Last Offices. For the author it was always a privilege and the patients she cared for at death are never forgotten in her prayers.
They are long remembered.

EARLY BEGINNINGS

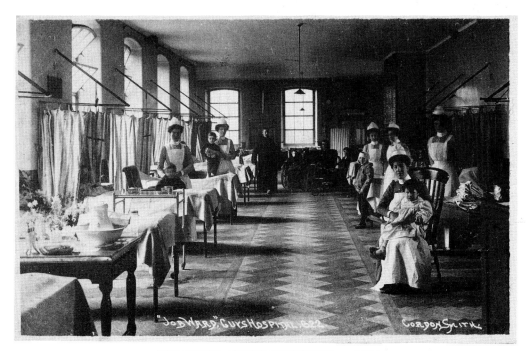

JOB WARD, GUY'S HOSPITAL, c. 1910
Nursing really began with monks and nuns offering hospitality for the sick in their monasteries
and convents. St. Bartholomew's is said to be the oldest hospital in England, founded in 1123,
followed soon after by St. Thomas's Hospital. Guy's Hospital was founded in 1721 by
Thomas Guy, who was a City bookseller and a leading governor of St. Thomas's Hospital.
Guy's opened in 1725 with 435 beds. Much of the old building remains today even though parts
of it were damaged by bombs in World War 2. Since the war, additions to the building include
a new surgical block and large tower block.

FLORENCE NIGHTINGALE.
Reproduced by J. Palmer Clarke, Cambridge (by permission).

FLORENCE NIGHTINGALE, c. 1905
The world owes much to Miss Nightingale. She was the founder of nursing as a profession and a pioneer of hospital reform. She became a nurse despite family opposition. In 1854, during the Crimean War, together with a party of 38 hospital nurses and 10 Roman Catholic nuns who were trained nurses, she set off for Scutari Hospital. She was known as "The Lady with the Lamp" because, on night duty, she would pass from bed to bed carrying her lamp. Florence soon realised that more men died from disease and insanitary conditions than from their wounds. On her return to London she established the Nightingale Training School at St. Thomas's Hospital and demanded that nurses be sober, honest, punctual, quiet and clean. The image of nursing was raised and the job became a respectable one for a young lady.

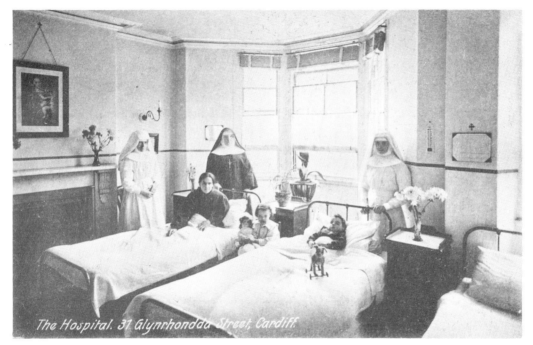

THE HOSPITAL, GLYNRHONDDA STREET, CARDIFF, c. 1905
This was one of the many hospitals founded by nuns, who interpret the nursing of the sick as an act of mercy. The famous Hospital of St. John and St. Elizabeth in London was founded by the Sisters of Charity. Today, many hospices are under the care of religious orders. St. Joseph's Hospice in Hackney has been caring for the terminally ill for several decades.

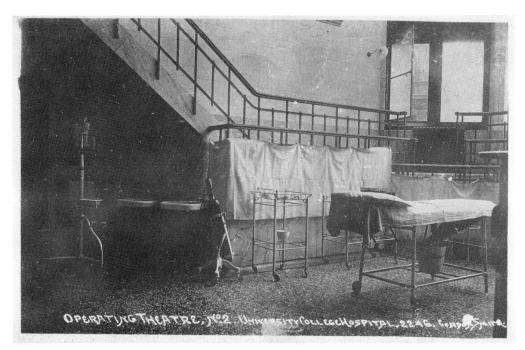

OPERATING THEATRE NO. 2, UNIVERSITY COLLEGE HOSPITAL, c. 1904
With advances in medical science, hospitals grew and many new ones were founded. University College Hospital, the famous London teaching hospital established in the early nineteenth century, was the first hospital to use ether for the amputation of a leg. Just a year later, chloroform was discovered and was found to be a better anaesthetic. However, more patients died as a result of infection than shock. Joseph Lister was the pioneer of antiseptic surgery and it was his use of carbolic acid - first used as a dressing on wounds in Glasgow Royal Infirmary in 1865 - that was responsible for the reduction in post-operative mortality.

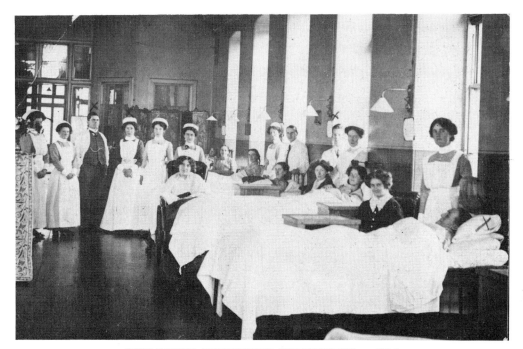

THE ROYAL INFIRMARY, EDINBURGH, c. 1910
The message on this postcard reads: "The bed marked X is the one I am now in. The chap I have marked with the X is the Dr I like best. He is tall and <u>red</u> headed. He lifts you on to the trolley when you go away to go thro. your operation. The young Dr next to him is the one who gives the chloroform. The other one marked X is the house surgeon and the Sister. There was a wee baby brought into our ward the other day severely burned, it only lived 2 hours. Poor wee thing". The card was sent by Sarah on Ward 14.

TEN POUNDS A YEAR AND ONE DAY OFF A MONTH

NURSES TRAINING SCHOOL, ST. MARY ABBOTT'S HOSPITAL, c. 1910
Anne O'Neill (aunt of the author) is on the left, at the back, leaning against the radiator. She is photographed here, aged 20, at the start of her three years training, at the end of which she would be expected to Staff for a year, in gratitude to the hospital for her training. Despite modernisation, the wards that Anne walked still exist today. A few years later, this young probationer would be nursing cholera cases worse than any text-book could describe.
(see pages 27 and 79)

ORATORY NURSES' HOME, PLAISTOW

THE ORATORY, NURSES' HOME, PLAISTOW, c. 1914

The message on this card reads: "Dear Hestie, this is the chapel where I am seated at 7.00 a.m. for prayers so you will see I am out of bed early..." It was the custom in some hospitals for Matron to lead her nurses in morning and evening prayers. Even as late as the mid-Fifties, my own training school, not a religious foundation, had very lengthy prayers each day of P.T.S. I do not think it made us better nurses.

MEN'S WARD, ASHTON-UNDER-LYNE DISTRICT INFIRMARY, c. 1908
Much of Anne's daily duty was spent in cleaning and other domestic work. This typical ward scene, complete with Sister's aspidistra plants, shows the wooden floor shining like glass. Notice the medicine trolley on the left. There were far fewer medicines than we have today and, of course, no antibiotics, but some of these early medicines were very effective. The watchful ward clock ticks on through the long, hard, busy day.

St. Thomas's Hospital
Casualty Waiting Hall.

THE CASUALTY WAITING HALL, ST. THOMAS'S HOSPITAL, c. 1905
The young probationer, Anne, would spend periods of time in various wards and departments.
St. Thomas's Hospital has early foundations in the Priory of St. Mary Overie, dating from 1106,
since when the lame, sick and lepers have been cared for. The original hospital was founded at
Southwark and, in 1868, moved to Lambeth to new buildings that were designed by
Henry Currey. These beautiful old buildings, overlooking the River Thames, never fail to
impress any visitor to London. The benches may be hard and the waiting may be long, but the
patients love "Tommy's".

THE LONDON HOSPITAL, c. 1914
England's largest hospital, known as the Great General Hospital for East London, was founded by a group of Christian subscribers who met in a tavern in Cheapside. In 1740, the hospital opened in a small house in Featherstone Street, which was rented at £16 per annum. In 1748, it moved to its new building in Whitechapel Road and has been enlarged at various times since. Despite bombing in the area in World War 2, much of the original building exists, especially the very interesting main entrance. The postcard shows the nurse's garden, known as the "Garden of Eden" by the London nurses. These happy probationers say that it was not "all work and no play".

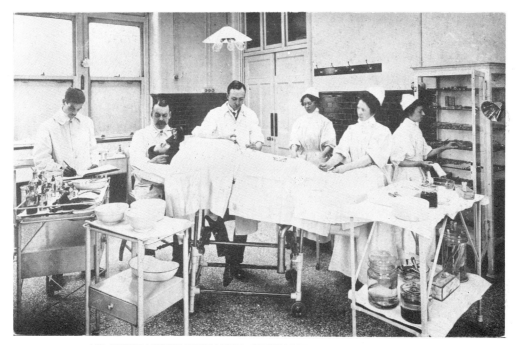

AN OPERATING THEATRE, UNKNOWN LOCATION, c. 1905

Not many nurses liked the idea of working in the theatre, as a junior's work was mostly cleaning and scrubbing. Her most important jobs were to keep out of Sister's way and be ready to catch any instruments that bad-tempered surgeons would throw on the floor! This scene is very different from today. None of the staff are wearing masks or gloves and, without antibiotics, there was a constant battle against infection. Sadly, patients often survived the dreaded operation only to succumb to subsequent infection. Sometimes even fairly complicated operations were performed at home on the kitchen table but, first, "a fire is laid and the floor well scrubbed".

Children's Ward,
The Hospital, Worthing.

CHILDREN'S WARD, THE HOSPITAL, WORTHING, c. 1910
A necessary part of any nurse's training is experience nursing children. Operations were performed similar to the type that a child would have today - repairs of hare-lip and cleft palate - although, of course, results were not as good as nowadays. The usual childhood complaints of appendicitis, tonsils and adenoids were also high on the list. This seems to be a fairly happy ward - notice the doll's pram and large teddy-bear. There are some delightful pictures of children on the walls and, either side of the door, portraits of King Edward VII and Queen Alexandra.

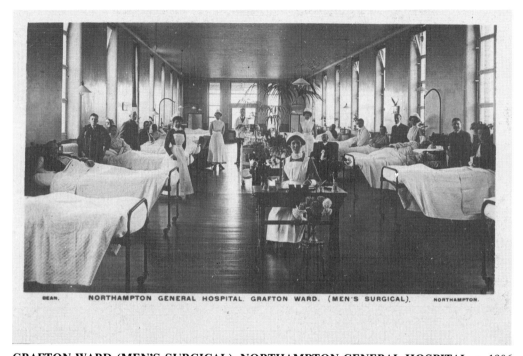

GRAFTON WARD (MEN'S SURGICAL), NORTHAMPTON GENERAL HOSPITAL, c. 1906
It would be a proud day when Anne (see page 14) would sit at her Sister's desk. Following experience in medical and surgical wards - both male and female, casualty and out-patients department, if Anne passed her examinations she would become a Trained Nurse.
State Registration of nurses started in 1919. As a Sister, she would have a slight increase in her very low pay and would have full responsibility for her ward. Northampton General Hospital was founded in 1743 and now has 681 beds.

21

SPECIALIST AND DIFFERENT HOSPITALS

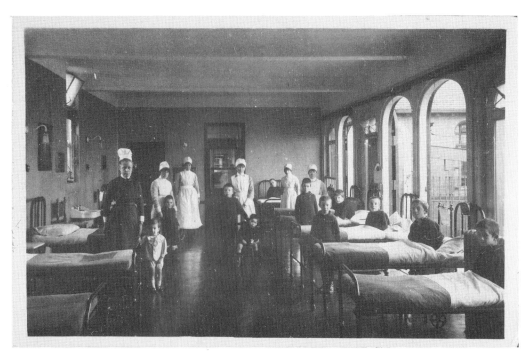

A WARD SCENE, UNKNOWN CHILDREN'S HOSPITAL, c. 1912
Hospitals often catered for a particular illness. Wards were kept strictly male or female. Children had their own hospitals and the oldest known such hospital in England is The Royal Manchester Children's Hospital, founded in 1829. This postcard is probably of the Queen's Hospital for Children, Hackney, and shows a boy's ward. The smart little boy holding Sister's hand has "watched the birdie" for quite long enough now! Most of the pictures of these early ward scenes are posed photographs.

THE NORTH LODGE, RAINHILL MENTAL HOSPITAL, LANCASHIRE, c. 1912

Not the sort of postcard one would want to adorn a mantelpiece! Few postcards of mental hospitals exist. Often, a mental hospital would be built miles away - out of sight and out of mind - in the country. Bethlem Royal Hospital for the insane, commonly known as Bedlam asylum, is our oldest hospital for the mentally sick. The original building was erected in 1812-15 and now houses the Imperial War Museum in its central portion. The wings were demolished when the hospital was transferred to new buildings near Croydon in 1930.

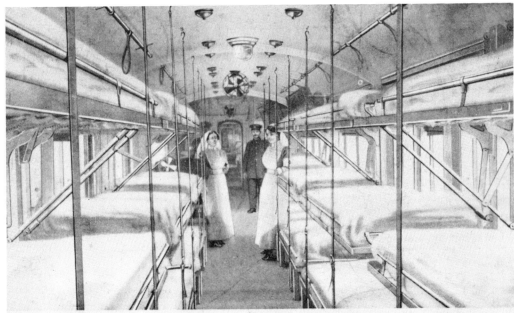

Interior of one of the Ward Cars of the Ambulance Train, constructed by the Caledonian Railway Company, on the order of the War Office, for conveyance of Wounded British Soldiers in France from the Front to the Sea-board.

A WARD CAR, CALEDONIAN RAILWAY AMBULANCE TRAIN, c. 1915

The full caption on this postcard reads: Interior of one of the Ward Cars of the Ambulance Train, constructed by the Caledonian Railway Company, on the order of the War Office, for conveyance of Wounded British Soldiers in France from the Front to the Sea-board".

In this ward, army nursing sisters, nurses and VADs nursed the wounded men. It was quite difficult as the train was moving most of the timè but, because of these "Cars", many men's lives were saved and some men recovered sufficiently to return to the Front.

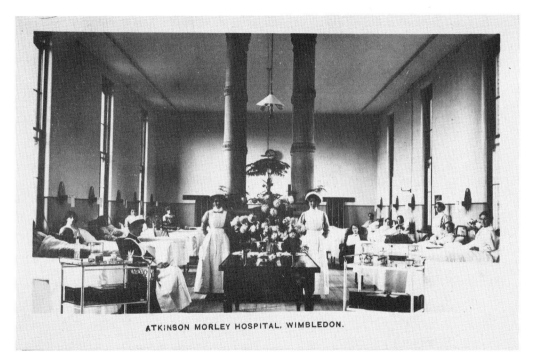

ATKINSON MORLEY HOSPITAL, WIMBLEDON.

ATKINSON MORLEY HOSPITAL, WIMBLEDON, c. 1905
The Hospital is famous nationally and world-wide for advanced excellence in brain surgery on
both children and adults. It also offers specialist rehabilitation for such patients.
The postcard shows a women's ward.

THE CANCER HOSPITAL, FULHAM ROAD, c. 1908
So sad was Doctor Marsden when his young wife died of cancer, that he decided to raise funds
for a special hospital for cancer patients which was established in 1851. The buildings seen on
this postcard were erected between 1859 and 1885. It is now known as the Royal Marsden
Hospital and has a famous children's branch in Surrey. This is a world-famous hospital for
those suffering from cancer. Notice the horse-drawn bus on the left.

H.M. HOSPITAL SHIP "OXFORDSHIRE."

H.M. HOSPITAL SHIP "OXFORDSHIRE", c. 1912
This fine ship was called to service two days before the start of World War 1. She carried the wounded from France to England and then served in the Dardanelles. This ship was a hospital, complete with operating theatre, and was staffed by Trained Nurses and VADs, St. John's Ambulance Brigade and Red Cross volunteers. Was Anne O'Neill (see page 14), now a Q.A.I.M.N.S. (Queen Alexandra's Imperial Military Nursing Service) Nursing Sister, on this ship with her wounded patients from Gallipoli? For her extreme devotion to duty, in nursing the typhoid and dysentery cases, Anne was awarded the Royal Red Cross medal.

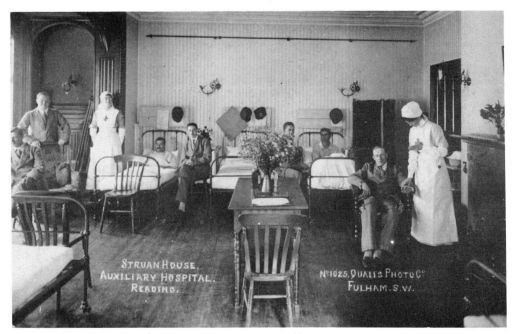

STRUAN HOUSE AUXILIARY HOSPITAL, READING, c. 1916

Following the dreadful battle of the Somme, there were so many wounded soldiers returning from France that the hospitals were full. Consequently, stately homes, large country houses, schools and some village halls were set up as emergency hospitals. Look around and you may see a plaque on a village hall reading: "This tablet records that during the Great War this village hall was used as a temporary hospital and 202 servicemen were nursed here". In the picture, the nurse on the left is a volunteer nurse.

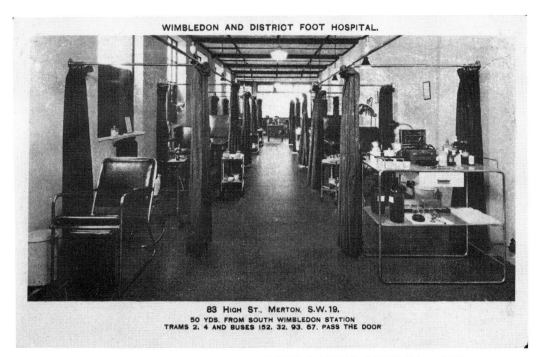

WIMBLEDON AND DISTRICT FOOT HOSPITAL.

83 High St., Merton, S.W.19.
50 YDS. FROM SOUTH WIMBLEDON STATION
TRAMS 2, 4 AND BUSES 152, 32, 93, 67. PASS THE DOOR

WIMBLEDON AND DISTRICT FOOT HOSPITAL, MERTON, c. 1920
No other reference to a specialist foot hospital can be found - and this one is now extinct.
With sore, diseased feet, one cannot walk and the whole body is affected. Corns, overgrown
toe-nails and infected nail-beds were some of the problems that would have been treated here.
The postcard was intended to advertise the hospital's services and, beneath the picture, has
information about access by public transport.

NEW WARD, WESTERN FEVER HOSPITAL, EARLS COURT, c. 1908

Such a specialist establishment was known as the Fever or Isolation Hospital. It was a good idea to nurse infections and fevers in a special hospital so as to avoid the spread of infection. Childbed or Puerperal fevers would also be treated here. Lectures on the control of infection started at this hospital in 1891. Higher, cleaner standards of housing, better nutrition and immunisation have almost eradicated diphtheria, scarlet fever and whooping-cough.

GAS EXTRACTION ROOM,
c. 1908

"Dear mother, this is where I had my teeth extracted by gas all fine, I had 5 out and I have to have 5 more out next Tuesday. Ask Fred what he thinks. Keep this card for your collection. Lizzie", reads the message, written on 16th December, 1909. I wonder what Fred thought? Luckily, Mother kept this card. Unfortunately, the location of this room is not given on the postcard, but it is possibly the Royal Dental Hospital, founded in 1858, which is situated in Leicester Square.

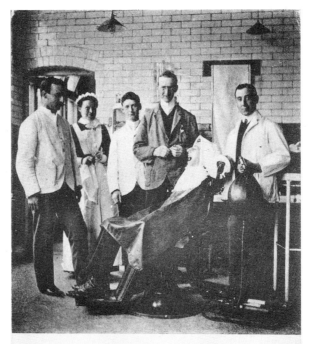

Gas Extraction Room

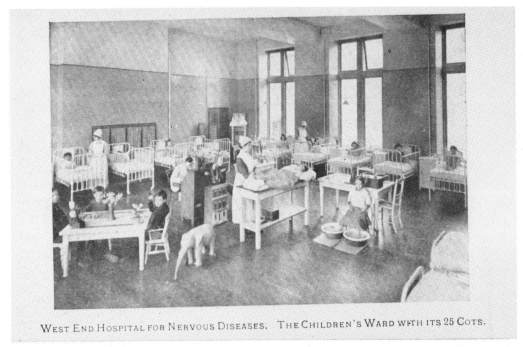

WEST END HOSPITAL FOR NERVOUS DISEASES. THE CHILDREN'S WARD WITH ITS 25 COTS.

THE CHILDREN'S WARD, WEST END HOSPITAL FOR NERVOUS DISEASES, c. 1906
Epilepsy, other forms of fit and, what is known today as certain behaviourial disorders, would
have been treated at this hospital. Modern drugs can now control many such complaints. This
ward, with its 25 cots, shows some form of early electrical massage therapy to the little girl's
feet, on the right of the picture. She certainly does not look at all happy and is very glum about
the whole treatment which, in the 1980s, appears to be rather weird and mysterious!

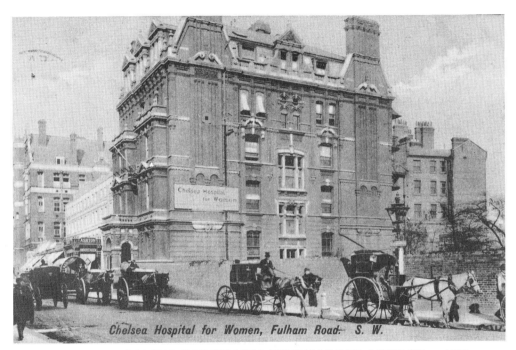

Chelsea Hospital for Women, Fulham Road. S. W.

CHELSEA HOSPITAL FOR WOMEN, FULHAM ROAD, LONDON, c. 1908
The Hospital was founded to treat diseases peculiar to women. It still occupies the same site but, unlike the view, now has a constant stream of noisy traffic outside and jet aircraft overhead. Other hospitals exist solely for women: The Elizabeth Garrett Anderson and Royal Free Hospitals which, until quite recently, were staffed by women doctors only.

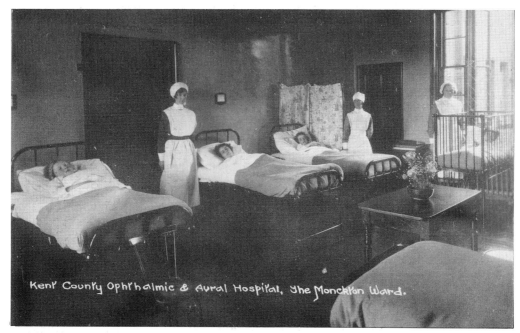

Kent County Ophthalmic & Aural Hospital, The Monckton Ward.

THE MONKTON WARD, KENT COUNTY OPHTHALMIC AND AURAL HOSPITAL, c. 1911
The nursing of eye patients needs special skill as, often, the patient is blindfolded with bandaging. Ear patients could be suffering from infected or "running" ears, which often led to infection of the ear-bone - a very painful condition. Surgical intervention helped but, without the "wonder-drug" penicillin or other germ-killers, recovery was slow. The patients in this picture are perhaps a little too tightly wrapped up. Notice the screens which would be moved from bed to bed to afford privacy; it was hard work pushing noisy screens up and down the ward. Compare this scene to Guy's (page 9) which was a wealthier hospital and provided individual screening around each bed.

The Hospital for Sick Children, Great Ormond Street, London. Annie Zunz Ward.

ANNIE ZUNZ WARD, THE HOSPITAL FOR SICK CHILDREN, GREAT ORMOND STREET, LONDON, c. 1920

This world-famous hospital has continued on the same site since its foundation in 1852. In 1929, James Barrie gave the Hospital the full copyright of his story, "Peter Pan". Peggy, who sent this postcard, is in the picture - the nurse on the right - and on 24th February, 1923, writes: "frightfully busy and we've stopped having "nights off" again. Shall be awfully sorry to leave the children". As a pupil midwife, the author remembers delivering a baby that needed immediate surgery. The new-born baby, his mother and the author were rushed through London by ambulance to Great Ormond Street, where they were able to save the baby's life.

35

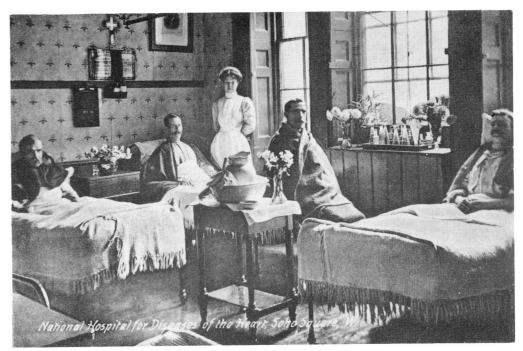

**NATIONAL HOSPITAL FOR DISEASES FOR THE HEART, SOHO SQUARE,
LONDON,** c. 1910

What great advances in heart surgery have been made since this picture was taken. Would the
surgeons of their day ever have dreamed that such things were possible? Notice the
religious text on the wall - maybe it read "Prepare to meet thy God". Why do the nurses on
most of these postcards look so solemn? Is it that they were all so tired from the long hours of
duty on their feet?

AN EARLY MOTOR AMBULANCE, c. 1912

This smart ambulance was presented by the British Steel Smelters' Mill, Iron, Tinplate and Kindred Trades Association, English Districts, to the British Red Cross Society and the St. John Ambulance Association. In earlier days it would have been a horse-drawn ambulance that would take people to hospital. This well-equipped vehicle was staffed by volunteers and the patient would pay according to his means. Some would come to hospital via the casualty department and others by an appointment - when a bed was vacant. Hospital waiting lists existed even in those days.

OUT-PATIENTS, ST. BARTHOLOMEW'S HOSPITAL, LONDON, c. 1899
On close examination of this example of very early flashlight photography, one can read the names of the doctors' clinics being held at that time. The staff, who are standing in the background are, from left to right: Evans, a porter; Herbert, a porter; Dr. Reichwold, house physician; Nurse Birch and Nurse Senior - their names have been marked on the reverse of the postcard. The doctor at the clinic would decide upon admission if needed. After a stay in hospital, the patient would be followed up to see that all was well. Throughout the patient's stay, the porters provide a most valuable, often undervalued, service.

THE KITCHEN, LEWISHAM HOSPITAL, c. 1912

Throughout the patient's stay, he or she will need feeding - and who cooks for all the other workers in a busy hospital? It was not only nurses and doctors, but also porters, clerks, laundry staff and a host of others, working both day and night. At St. Thomas's, one of the Almoners always attended at meal times to see that "rations were ample and properly cooked". Ward meal times were always a great ritual, served with punctuality. The dishes on the table in the right foreground contain a mixture of salads. On the centre table are the containers for the various wards - Maternity, Bristow, Allenby and Cavell.

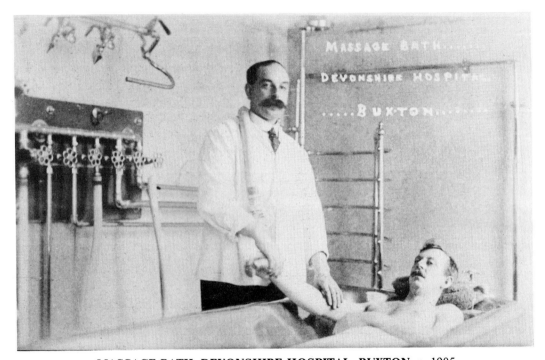

MASSAGE BATH, DEVONSHIRE HOSPITAL, BUXTON, c. 1905
The soothing, beneficial effects of water on the body have been known since earliest
times - hence the popularity of today's spa-baths and hydrotherapy pools. However, this patient
does not seem to be enjoying his treatment!

A WARD SCENE, UNKNOWN LOCATION, c. 1910

At all times the ward would be spick and span. Nurses were forever hurrying under the ticking
clock. For the doctor's round, it was silence. Very few hospitals had screens around each bed,
so the noisy screens would be dragged up and down the ward all day. As late as the mid-Fifties,
the author remembers the constant back-aching screen-pulling. It was a very long day for the
patient. The ward was fully-aired at all times - notice the open windows - as even the best of
wards could be smelly places. Notice the young double leg amputee sitting in the wheelchair.

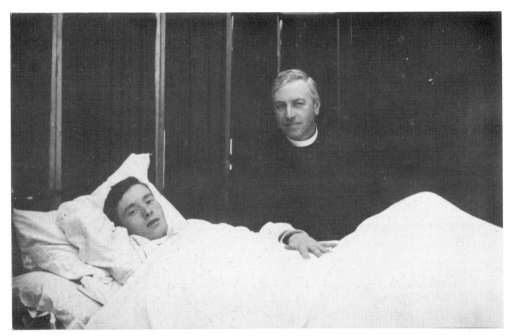

THE HOSPITAL CHAPLAIN, UNKNOWN LOCATION, c. 1913
Each hospital had its own chapel and the hospital chaplains would visit patients regularly.
A chaplain's duty was not only to the patients but also to the patients' relatives and the hospital
staff. His day might begin with prayers and a service in the chapel then a visit to the wards
where he may have to comfort a nurse, crying following a death of a child, or say prayers for
the recovery of a patient. His final duty would be to anoint the dying. Chaplains, of whatever
religion or faith, were, and are, always regarded with high esteem in any hospital.

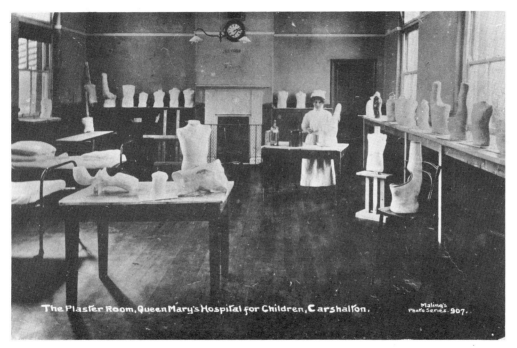

**THE PLASTER ROOM, QUEEN MARY'S HOSPITAL FOR CHILDREN,
CARSHALTON,** c. 1915

One's hospital treatment may require a plaster cast which is used to correct or prevent a
deformity. On this postcard, dated 17th December 1916, Edith Ross writes: "...I've got heaps to
do preparing for one thing and the other. Our concert is Christmas week, I'm in it", and she
also asks her mother, a Mrs. Ross in Scotland, to send "some evergreens for the ward,
before Christmas".

The picture on the cover of this book is also of this hospital.

MATERNITY HOSPITALS

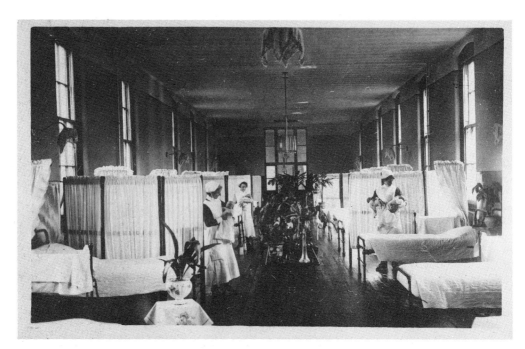

WARD F6, UNKNOWN LOCATION, c. 1905

According to the information written on the reverse of the card, this was the Labour Ward and the nursing staff, from left to right, are Sister Marshall, a pupil nurse, and Sister Walker, the midwife. This is possibly Queen Charlotte's Hospital, which was in central London but is now in Hammersmith, the oldest maternity hospital, founded in 1739. Because Queen Victoria agreed to take pain-relieving chloroform, childbirth gradually became less painful. However, a text-book for midwives, dated 1908, has no mention of any pain-relief for the mother-to-be! In 1900, many babies died soon after birth.

Baby Incubators. Crystal Palace. Child Life Section.

BABY INCUBATORS, CHILD LIFE SECTION, CRYSTAL PALACE EXHIBITION, c. 1908
At the Great Exhibition of 1908, Britain showed off its invention to the world. The incubator
developed from a padded box or a padded basket, with the baby being wrapped in blankets,
surrounded by hot water bottles to keep the temperature at 90°F. The incubators saved many
premature babies' lives, although, at first, few hospitals could afford one like those on show at
the Exhibition. There were real babies in these incubators! The advertisements are for
Wright's Coal Tar Soap and Mellin's Food.

45

One !

ONE!

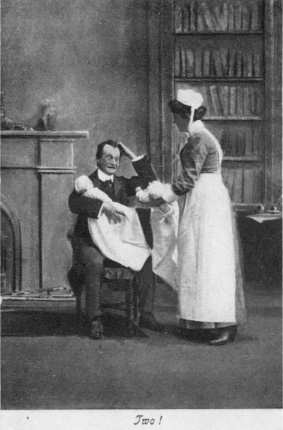

Two !

TWO!

THREE!

Poor dad! What a shock! He is happy to receive one little mite, two is a problem, somewhat, but - the thought and site of triplets!!! There was no Family Allowance or Welfare State in the early 1900s.
This is a set of three cards published by Valentines, circa 1905:

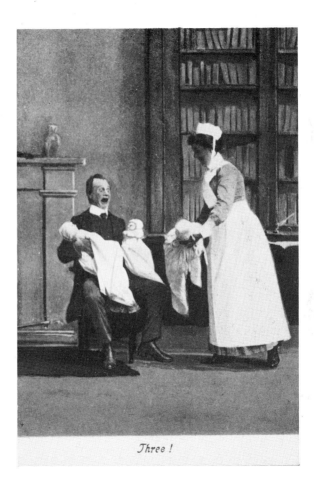

Three !

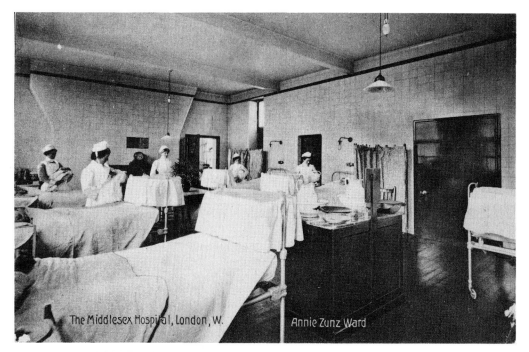

The Middlesex Hospital, London, W. Annie Zunz Ward

ANNIE ZUNZ WARD, THE MIDDLESEX HOSPITAL, c. 1910
The Middlesex had several maternity wards and the writer of this postcard tells us that this is
"where the mothers were convalescent". This was the first general hospital to have a "lying in"
ward, in 1747, for the reception and immediate relief of indigent soldiers' and sailors' wives.
Maternity cases were not admitted to the Infirmaries in the early days.

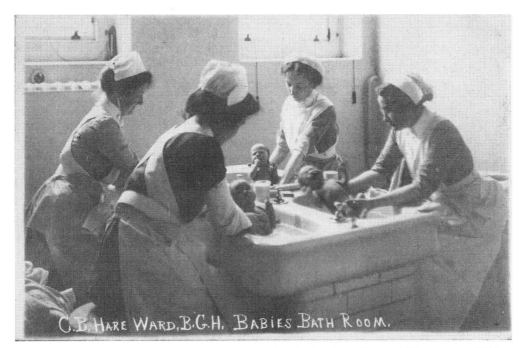

C.B. HARE WARD. B.G.H. BABIES BATH ROOM.

BABIES' BATH ROOM, G.B. HARE WARD, BRISTOL GENERAL HOSPITAL, c. 1910
Each pupil, that is a Trained Nurse training to be a midwife, would be given at least six babies to bath. What beautiful babies they are! Women were expected to "lie in" for several days after giving birth, but for poorer women with other children this was often quite impossible.

FUND RAISING

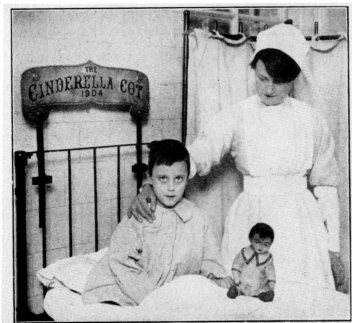

Must We Turn the Mothers and Children Away?

THE QUEEN'S HOSPITAL FOR CHILDREN, HACKNEY ROAD, LONDON, c. 1905
Before the establishment of the National Health Service, every hospital had to be funded by public donations and subscriptions. Each hospital was entirely self-supporting and relied on the generosity of the community it served. Due to poverty, many children suffered from a painful bone complaint - osteomalacia (rickets) - and, without modern-day antibiotics, they were rarely healed. The Queen's is now with the Great Ormond Street group of hospitals. This interesting postcard would have been used to appeal for donations towards the £35,000 needed to finance the hospital each year.

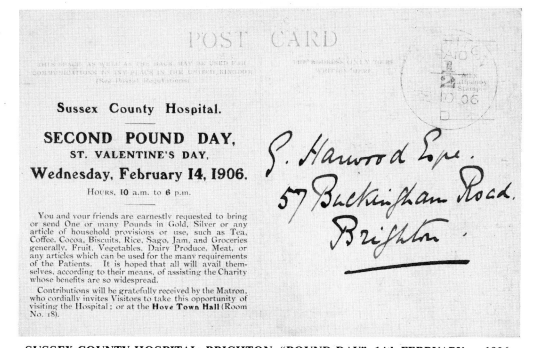

POST CARD

Sussex County Hospital.

SECOND POUND DAY,
ST. VALENTINE'S DAY,
Wednesday, February 14, 1906.

Hours, 10 a.m. to 6 p.m.

You and your friends are earnestly requested to bring or send One or many Pounds in Gold, Silver or any article of household provisions or use, such as Tea, Coffee, Cocoa, Biscuits, Rice, Sago, Jam, and Groceries generally, Fruit, Vegetables, Dairy Produce, Meat, or any articles which can be used for the many requirements of the Patients. It is hoped that all will avail themselves, according to their means, of assisting the Charity whose benefits are so widespread.

Contributions will be gratefully received by the Matron, who cordially invites Visitors to take this opportunity of visiting the Hospital; or at the **Hove Town Hall** (Room No. 18).

SUSSEX COUNTY HOSPITAL, BRIGHTON, "POUND DAY", 14th FEBRUARY, c. 1906
What an ingenious way of fund raising - to give a pound of whatever you want from gold to garden peas! It is certain that Matron would have written to former patients and to those in the locality who were known for their generosity. On "Pound Day", Matron was available to receive contributions and visitors could look round the hospital. Other suggestions for suitable donations included tea, coffee, rice, jam, sago or any articles suitable for patients. The picture side of the card shows Peel Ward and gives the number of in-patients for 1905 - 2,145 and out-patients - 8,765.

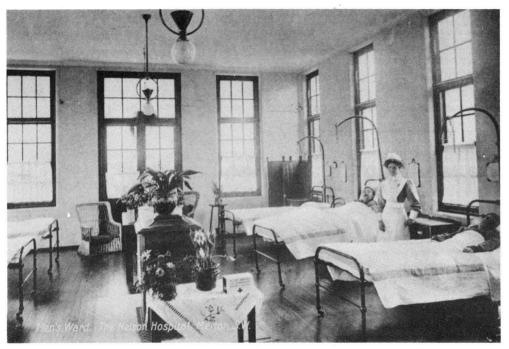

MEN'S WARD, THE NELSON HOSPITAL, MERTON, c. 1906
The odd collecting box was placed in entrance halls and, as in the picture, on the central
ward table. It was a sad day for so many, when hospitals that had for years been entirely
dependent on local charity and donations, were taken over by the Welfare State.
Years-old minute books closed as the final Voluntary Hospital Management Committees
met in 1948.

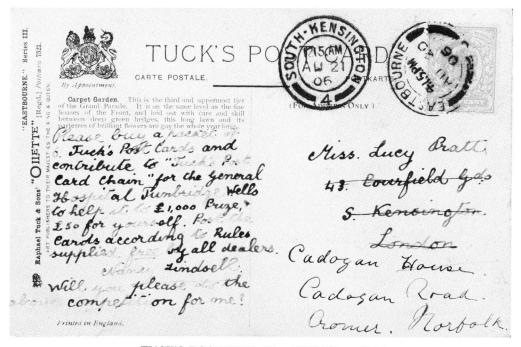

TUCK'S POSTCARD, 21st AUGUST, c. 1906

Raphael Tuck & Sons, well-known publishers of picture postcards, encouraged fund raising for hospitals. This card was part of a "Tuck's Post Card Chain" to raise £1,000 for a hospital of one's choice - in this case the General Hospital, Tunbridge Wells. This was a considerable sum at that time. Other hospitals sold their own cards showing ward scenes as a form of advertising and, also, the purchasers paid a halfpenny extra on the card, for the hospital funds. However, a card from a hospital was not as popular as a seaside scene for Aunt Matilda's album.

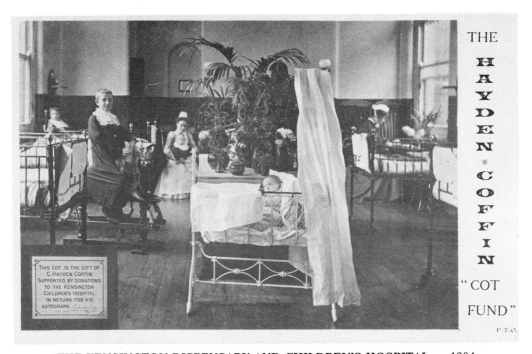

THE H A Y D E N * C O F F I N "COT FUND"

P.T.O.

THIS COT IS THE GIFT OF
C. HAYDEN COFFIN.
SUPPORTED BY DONATIONS
TO THE KENSINGTON
CHILDREN'S HOSPITAL
IN RETURN FOR HIS
AUTOGRAPH.

THE KENSINGTON DISPENSARY AND CHILDREN'S HOSPITAL, c. 1904
In some older wards one can see well-polished brass plates one hundred years old, with
the name of a generous benefactor shining out in memory of a loved one.
Commemorations are similar too: "From the owner and workers of the Wool Mill"; "An
anonymous donor"; "In memory of David Lyell, Second Lieutenant 7th Battalion Royal
Scots, killed in action 12th July 1915". The cot in the picture is funded by donations
given for the autograph of the then famous actor, Mr. C. Hayden Coffin, with a
minimum donation of 2/6d. The General Infirmary at Leeds rescued some plaques when
wards were updated and they now have place of honour in the new entrance hall.

THE FIREMAN'S DOG, c. 1907
The British are known for their
love of animals and few could
walk past "Jack" or other
collecting dogs. "Jack" collected
almost £150 for the hospitals of
Sussex. Other dogs, famous for
their collecting, have also been
remembered on postcards.

THE FIREMAN'S DOG, WHO HAS COLLECTED
NEARLY £150 FOR THE HOSPITALS.

"JACK'S" PLEA.

I plead for those, who, in the hour of pain, ask for release,
With science aiding Nature to regain their health and ease.
Although you now from painful ills are free and laugh at fears,
The time may come, an inmate you will be in future years,
So help my box to fill, emptied so free for one and all,
And "Jack's" brown eyes will dance with glee as the pence fall:

M.B.F.B., Tun. Wells.

INFIRMARY SUNDAY, BALBY, YORKSHIRE, c. 1908
Infirmary Sunday was held annually in April, when all the church collections went to the
hospitals. Special fêtes, parades, sales and events, such as the one pictured here, took
place. Even the poorest families gave to their hospital and an Annual Report of 1904
states: "Mrs. Lindsay - old clothes", such a gift would be useful even if only used for
cleaning rags. Another gift: "Lipton Limited, Kirkgate - a cake (Leith Hospital)".
Gifts continue to this day but it is more likely to be a television set, or other item of
modern equipment, given by the League of Friends.

ON THE DISTRICT

THE QUEEN'S NURSE, c. 1930
From the 17th century there are reports of visiting nurses; nuns, St. Vincent de Paul and some infirmaries providing a service to the community. In 1859, William Rathbone was so impressed by the Trained Nurse he employed to look after his dying wife at home, that, at his own expense, he paid for the nurse to continue to nurse the sick poor in their own homes. With £70,000 from the Jubilee Fund, the Queen Victoria Jubilee Institute for Nurses was founded. Its aim was to provide specially trained nurses, with additional experience, to nurse the sick in their own homes. The full caption on this card reads: "Naturally, a Queen's Nurse is looked upon as a never-failing source of information on the care and feeding of babies - and she never fails to help."

NATURALLY, A QUEEN'S NURSE IS LOOKED UPON AS A NEVER-FAILING SOURCE OF INFORMATION ON THE CARE AND FEEDING OF BABIES - AND SHE NEVER FAILS TO HELP

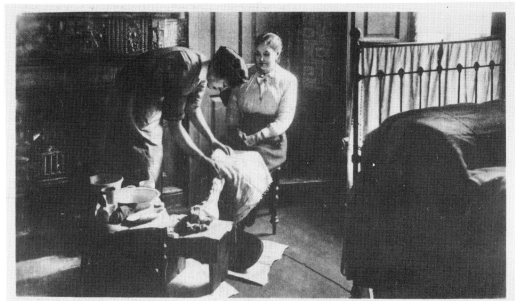

"THAT'S MUCH EASIER, THANK YOU, NURSE!" AN EVERYDAY EVENT IN THE LIFE OF A QUEEN'S NURSE DURING HER ROUND OF VISITS TO HUMBLE HOMES.

THE QUEEN'S NURSE, c. 1930

The full caption here reads: " 'That's much easier, thank you, Nurse!' An everyday event in the life of a Queen's Nurse during her round of visits to humble homes".
From further sums of money, District Nursing developed. In 1925, Queen Mary succeeded as Patron and the name was changed to The Queen's Institute of Nursing. On passing an examination, every Queen's Nurse is given an individual roll number. Dame Rosalind Paget became Queen's Nurse No. 1 in 1890. The author became Queen's Nurse No. 279974 in September 1961. A patient's home can be a castle, caravan, high-rise flat, boat, ordinary house or tent - the Queen's Nurse is always an honoured guest.

VICTORIA NURSES' HOME,
c. 1900

In this photograph, each Queen's Nurse is wearing her medal inscribed "Queen's Institute of District Nursing". Look at their pets, all posing for the cameraman. The armband worn by the nurse on the right, is known as a brassard and was worn by a senior nurse. Unfortunately, there is no indication of the location of this home. Inside, the black bags and other items of equipment would be kept. Articles for the comfort of the patient are loaned out. The Queen's Nurse, with her specialist training, would know where to obtain further help, or financial assistant from charities, for her patients.

BURY HOUSE NURSES INSTITUTE, EDMONTON, MIDDLESEX, c. 1904
On another card of this building, a notice-board reads "Bury House Nurses Institute (established 1900) Visiting and Residential Nurses supplied for Medical and Surgical cases attended by doctors. Maternity Nurses for Residential work or daily visits. Maternity Branch 357 Fore St." This House was demolished in 1930.
In 1878, Coleman's of Norwich were the first employers to appoint a visiting Trained Nurse to see their sick employees.

"NOW OFF ON YOUR BIKE!",
c. 1900
The exact location of this photograph is unknown, but it was somewhere in the north of England. What a long skirt to cycle in! The Queen's Nurse was very often the very best friend to a patient. At the Centenary Service for the Queen's Nursing Institute in Westminster Abbey, in September 1987, The Right Hon. Robert Runcie, Archbishop of Canterbury, in his address said: " 'Here comes my best friend', said the Bangladeshi woman in Stepney, 'Enter the District Nurse' ".

WINTRY DAYS OFFER NO OBSTACLES TO THE NURSE IN THE PERFORMANCE OF HER DUTIES.

THE QUEEN'S NURSE, c. 1930

The full caption reads: "Wintry days offer no obstacles to the Nurse in the performance of her duties". The Queen's Nurse, out in all weathers, uses many different forms of transport: cycle, pony and trap, boat, car and even aeroplane but, most of all, her own two feet! She will always turn up, albeit late if very bad weather prevails. On the reverse of the card, a printed paragraph reads: "Please keep the ball rolling and help the fund. Buy a packet of these cards (6 for 1/-) and send to friends. To be obtained from Organising Headquarters......" They were issued by The Scottish National Memorial to Queen Alexandra. Other cards from the packet were shown on pages 57 and 58.

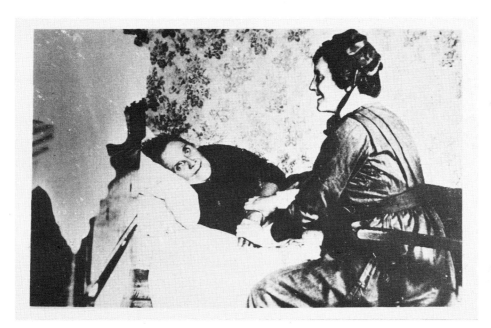

"THE HAPPIEST HOUR OF THE DAY", c. 1900
This picture sums it all up. True nursing as William Rathbone wished for his own dear
wife; the best of care for the poorest in their own homes. Sometimes, the Queen's Nurse
would be the only visitor to the frail, old and unloved. The total care of the
patient could mean putting food out for the cat; laying and lighting a fire - if there was
no-one else to do it, and anything else necessary for the patient's complete welfare.
"I was sick and you visited me".
(Picture reproduced courtesy Queen's Nursing Institute)

ANGELS AT THE FRONT

ON SERVICE

ON SERVICE, c. 1916
One of the many glamour-type
cards issued during
World War 1, this was painted
by Harold Copping in 1916.
There was a dreadful shortage of
nurses and, as fighting
progressed, more wounded were
brought home. It was the
volunteers who, after a very
short training, were faced with
the most gruesome tasks. Many
of these volunteers had come
from homes where they
themselves had been waited
upon. Often frowned on by
Trained Nurses, these VADs,
unpaid and overworked, were
truly the heroines of the war.

VAD, TENTERDEN, 1913

VAD stands for Voluntary Aid Detachment. In the early days, before World War 1, it was a respected thing for a young lady to spend some time each week learning about basic nursing and bandaging. Later on, when they were called to duty, it certainly was not a "bed of roses". For years, many VADs suffered crippling, damaged fingers caused by constant infections acquired when nursing the wounded.

NURSE EDITH CAVELL, ECOLE D'INFIRMIERES, 1912
Edith Louisa Cavell was born in 1865, the daughter of a Norfolk vicar. In this photograph, she is seen seated in the 2nd row, fourth from the left. She is wearing the uniform of Matron at this training school for nurses. At the outbreak of war, she was Matron at the Berkendael Medical Institute in Brussels and was later to be Matron of the British Red Cross Hospital in Brussels. Unlike most of the nurses featured in this section of the book, Nurse Cavell was a Trained Nurse, not a volunteer.

NURSE CAVELL, 1915
Nurse Cavell was arrested on 5th August by the German authorities and was executed on 12th October 1915, on a false charge of having assisted British, French and Belgian soldiers to escape. One of the martyrs of World War 1, she said "I am happy to die for my country". She is a great inspiration to all nurses at all times. So loved was she, that the nation erected a statue of her in St. Martin's Place, London. She was buried in the grounds of Norwich Cathedral.

This postcard was one of many issued in her memory. Her death caused a tremendous outcry and, shortly after, a recruiting campaign resulted in the enlisting of nearly twice as many volunteers as normal.

NURSE CAVELL

O! deed to blast a cruel coward's soul
And bring the race of Huns to deeper shame,
You yet have brought us nearer to our goal
For while our hearts still hold the martyr's name
We shall be given strength to wield the blade
In that dear cause for which her life was paid.
C.E.B in the London "Evening News"

NURSE EDITH CAVELL
"Executed" at Brussels, October, 1915.

7655-A.   ROTARY PHOTO. E.C.

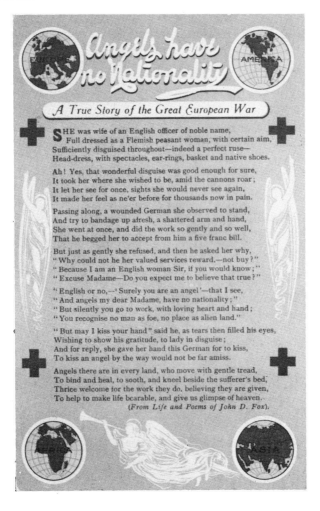

Angels have no Nationality

EUROPE   AMERICA

A True Story of the Great European War

SHE was wife of an English officer of noble name,
  Full dressed as a Flemish peasant woman, with certain aim,
Sufficiently disguised throughout—indeed a perfect ruse—
Head-dress, with spectacles, ear-rings, basket and native shoes.

Ah! Yes, that wonderful disguise was good enough for sure,
It took her where she wished to be, amid the cannons roar;
It let her see for once, sights she would never see again,
It made her feel as ne'er before for thousands now in pain.

Passing along, a wounded German she observed to stand,
And try to bandage up afresh, a shattered arm and hand,
She went at once, and did the work so gently and so well,
That he begged her to accept from him a five franc bill.

But just as gently she refused, and then he asked her why,
"Why could not he her valued services reward.—not buy?"
"Because I am an English woman Sir, if you would know;"
"Excuse Madame—Do you expect me to believe that true?"

"English or no,—' Surely you are an angel'—that I see,
"And angels my dear Madame, have no nationality;"
"But silently you go to work, with loving heart and hand;
"You recognise no man as foe, no place as alien land."

"But may I kiss your hand" said he, as tears then filled his eyes,
Wishing to show his gratitude, to lady in disguise;
And for reply, she gave her hand this German for to kiss,
To kiss an angel by the way would not be far amiss.

Angels there are in every land, who move with gentle tread,
To bind and heal, to sooth, and kneel beside the sufferer's bed;
Thrice welcome for the work they do, believing they are given,
To help to make life bearable, and give us glimpse of heaven.
                    (From Life and Poems of John D. Fox).

AFRICA   ASIA

ANGELS HAVE NO NATIONALITY, c. 1915
Many poems and songs, similar to this one, were written about VADs and nurses. Like Edith Cavell, a nurse treats all - regardless of class, creed or race - friend or foe, with the same standard of care and tenderness.
Besides Edith Cavell, other nurses died at enemy hands, in the course of their duty. One such nurse was Odette Malossane.

"OUR PRINCESS", c. 1915
As an encouragement to recruitment, H.R.H. Princess Mary, the daughter of King George V and Queen Mary, joined the Red Cross. In this picture, she is knitting - maybe a pair of soldier's socks! World-wide the Red Cross is a symbol of help to the injured and, at war, most fighting men would always respect the Red Cross.
(Published by Wildt & Kray)

W & K London   OUR PRINCESS.   No 116

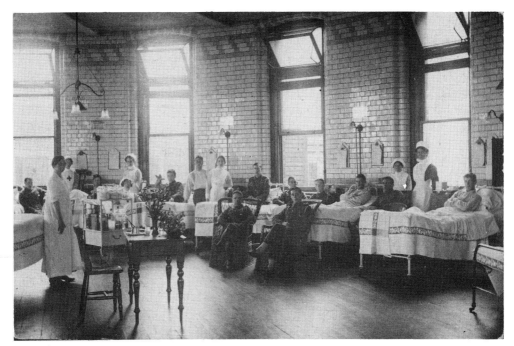

A WARD SCENE, UNKNOWN LOCATION, c. 1917

Here the VADs perform a valuable service in an unknown hospital, alongside the fully-trained staff. Only a week before, a young girl volunteer would have received a letter from Matron with the response: "Too young". Then, as the war's wounded filled the hospitals, she would have recieved a second letter with the urgent request: "Come tomorrow". This valuable service was formed in 1909 and VADs went to camp in 1914. Much of the menial hospital work - lighting fires, washing up, floor cleaning, etc, - was done by the humble volunteers, some of whom were only 17 years old.

A GLAMOUR CARD, c. 1915

Another card designed to encourage more women to volunteer. Many true stories of the heroism of VADs remain untold and the conditions they worked in, completely unpaid, were frequently appalling. Many a serviceman returned to the Front, thanks to the nursing care he received. A VAD normally had one year's training in England before going to France but, as the war progressed, VADs with only three months' training were sent abroad.

A FIELD AMBULANCE, c. 1915
This postcard shows the reality of battle. It was drawn by Harry Payne and his postcards
are very collectable; each card is a miniature work of art and the colours are superb.
"Stretcher bearers!" was the frequent cry. A wounded soldier was carried by stretcher to
the ambulance, then on to a nurse at the casualty clearing station or field hospital.

THE VOLUNTEERS

**STRETCHER PRACTICE, ST. JOHN'S AMBULANCE BRIGADE,
UNKNOWN LOCATION,** c. 1916

The St. John's Ambulance Brigade, founded in 1877, takes its name from the Knights Hospitallers of the Grand Priory of St. John of Jerusalem, one of the oldest orders of chivalry. Unpaid men and women train to be useful in an emergency, with a sound knowledge of first-aid. Today, there is a cadet section and those too young to join the Brigade learn basic first-aid and nursing and give many hours valuable service to the community. At any large public function the S.J.A.B. will be in attendance.

FRED SPURGIN

EVEN A LITTLE THING HELPS.

Un rien peut quelquefois servir a quelquechose.

"EVEN A LITTLE THING HELPS", c. 1915
Is she begging for money for Red Cross funds or is it appealing for even a little girl to join the VADs or Red Cross? This delightful postcard picture was drawn by Fred Spurgin and, as with many other cards of World War 1, has a caption in both English and French.
(Published by Inter-Art Co.)

A RED CROSS GROUP, UNKNOWN LOCATION, c. 1920
The Red Cross was founded in 1864 by Henri Dunant in Switzerland. The symbol was
the opposite of the Swiss flag - a red cross on a white background. The aim was
at the sign of the Red Cross, the war-wounded and their personnel would be protected
and military hospitals neutral. The British Red Cross Society started in 1876. All over
the country, B.R.C.S. members train for service in peace or war. Today, they run
day-centres, clubs for the handicapped, hospital visiting services and help with caring for
the aged and handicapped in the community - in addition to first-aid duties.
This postcard is thought to show a group in the Aylesbury area.

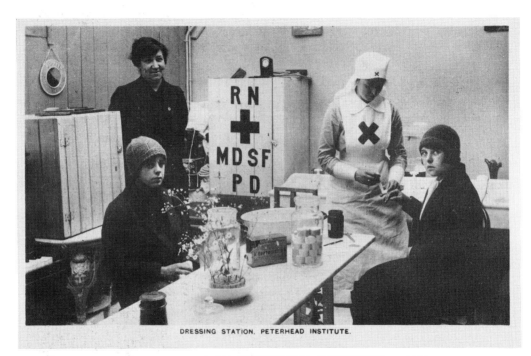

DRESSING STATION, PETERHEAD INSTITUTE.

DRESSING STATION, PETERHEAD INSTITUTE, c. 1921
Scotland has St. Andrew's Ambulance Association and thus wear the diagonal cross of
St. Andrew on their uniforms. Here, the St. Andrew's volunteer nurse is on duty at a
Royal National Mission to Deep Sea Fisherman Dressing Station. With no state help, it
relies entirely on voluntary contributions as do the S.J.A.B. and the B.R.C.S.
Notice the collecting box on the table.

S.J.A.B. NURSING MEMBER, UNKNOWN LOCATION, c. 1905
The armband denotes membership of the S.J.A.B. Before being allowed into uniform, stiff examinations in first-aid and nursing had to be passed. A pair of scissors was kept in the bag attached to the nurse's belt.

NURSE IN H.M. FORCES

MEDICAL & NURSING STAFF. N.C.O⁸ & MEN. ISOLATION HOSPITAL. ALDERSHOT.1915.

ISOLATION HOSPITAL, ALDERSHOT, c. 1915

The postcard shows the medical and nursing staff with several of the N.C.O.s and men.
The nurses in capes are known as Queen Alexandra's Imperial Nursing Service Sisters
and Staff Nurses. A corps of specialist nurses for the army was set up in 1881, it was
Queen Alexandra who designed their badges and she was proud to be their patron.
The Royal Air Force had its own nursing service, known as Princess Mary's Royal Air
Force Nursing Service, founded in 1918.

DEPARTURE OF SOME "TERRIERS" FOR MESOPOTAMIA, c. 1914
This is the message on the back of the card and the picture could possibly be of Queen
Mary's Military Hospital, Whalley, Lancashire, and maybe, one of the unidentified
nurses is Anne O'Neill (see page 14). Notice their long coats and outdoor uniforms. The
Territorial Force Nursing Service Reserve, founded in 1906, were commonly known as
the "Terriers". These were volunteer Trained Nurses, setting off to a very difficult
form of nursing; the men being seriously ill with typhoid and dysentery.

PHOTO:
EARLE HARRISON.

BRITISH RED CROSS FIELD AMBULANCE.

432 D.
BEAGLES POSTCARDS

WHICH IS QUIETLY PERFORMING SUCH HEROIC WORK, BRINGING WOUNDED SOLDIERS IN TO THE
FIELD HOSPITALS FROM THE FIGHTING LINE.

BRITISH RED CROSS FIELD AMBULANCE, c. 1917
The main job for the ambulance party was to bring wounded soldiers from the front to
the field hospitals. On the field, nurses often wore tin hats and khaki trousers.
This picture is obviously posed and the men's uniforms are immaculate. Notice the
well-equipped box and basket that have been opened to expose their contents for the
photographer.

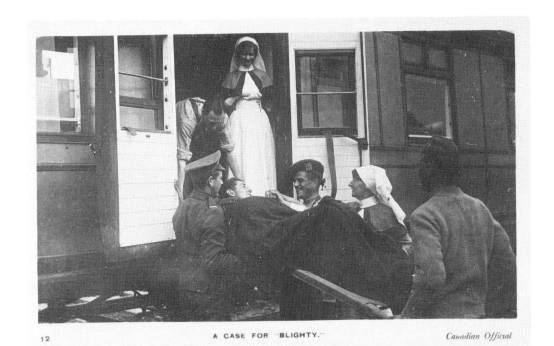

A CASE FOR "BLIGHTY."

Canadian Official

12

A CASE FOR "BLIGHTY", c. 1916
Many a wounded man would pray that he would be sent home to "Blighty".
The Royal Navy have their own nurses, also bearing Queen Alexandra's name, known as
Queen Alexandra's Royal Naval Nursing Service. This service started with a
Mrs. McKenzie taking 6 nursing sisters, employed by the Royal Navy, to a base hospital
at the start of the Crimean War; her action proved to be a great success. On this card, a
Q.A.R.N.N.S. Sister welcomes her patient aboard an ambulance train.

Q.A.I.M.N.S. MATRON AT HER DESK, UNKNOWN LOCATION
In any hospital, there is always plenty of paper work! The Q.A.'s uniform has changed little since 1914. Matron's hospital could be in any building from a church, school, stately home, town hall, village hall or tent, to a properly equipped hospital. The need for accommodation for the wounded was desperate. Matron and her Q.A.'s had to cope as best as they could. Sadly, many army nurses died of infections and some were shot by the enemy.

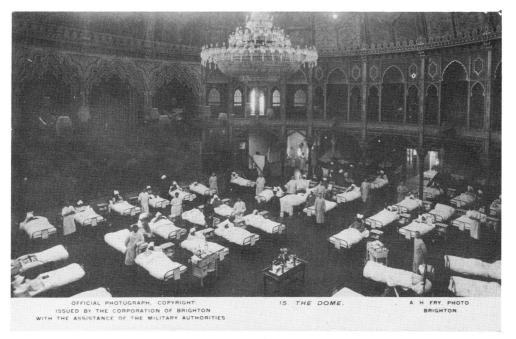

OFFICIAL PHOTOGRAPH. COPYRIGHT·
ISSUED BY THE CORPORATION OF BRIGHTON
WITH THE ASSISTANCE OF THE MILITARY AUTHORITIES

15. THE DOME.

A. H. FRY PHOTO
BRIGHTON

THE DOME, BRIGHTON, c. 1917

This was a very stately military hospital. As more and more wounded soldiers filled the makeshift hospitals, so more supplies were needed. Local people donated sheets, blankets, cutlery and even pots and pans. Many wounded Indian soldiers were nursed here at Brighton.

No 1 Theatre, Beaufort War Hospital, Fishponds, Bristol. 1480.

NO. 1 THEATRE, BEAUFORT WAR HOSPITAL, FISHPONDS, BRISTOL, c. 1917
Originally an asylum, this hospital was used for the increasing numbers of war casualties.
It is now known as Manor Park Hospital, Bristol.

PATIENTS. SISTER + NURSES OF (QUEEN MARY WARD) 2ND EASTERN GENERAL HOSPITAL BRIGHTON 191

QUEEN MARY WARD, 2ND EASTERN GENERAL HOSPITAL, BRIGHTON, c. 1915
This hospital was set up in the Brighton, Hove and Sussex Grammar School, Dyke Road,
Brighton. A notice on the school's railings advised pupils to reassemble at the
old premises.
On this postcard, Sister is posing with a group of her patients and nurses.

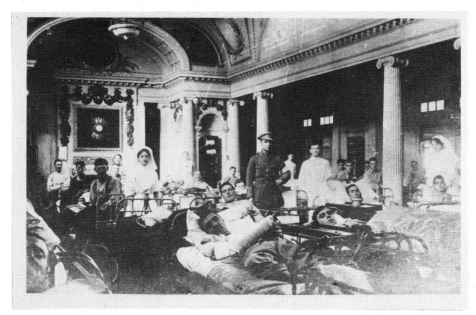

THE LOUNGE, "A" DECK, H.M. HOSPITAL SHIP "AQUITANIA", c. 1917
During the First World War, the "Aquitania", one of the world's largest passenger ships,
was requisitioned as a hospital ship - notice the elegant surroundings for the patients!
The war-wounded were being brought home and were in the care of Q.A.s, VADs, Red
Cross and S.J.A.B. nurses, who all served on these ships; some of these nurses took a
long time to get their "sea legs". A large red cross, visible to the enemy, was painted on
the ship's exterior to show that she was carrying wounded men. Sadly, many ships were
torpedoed and nurses and patients drowned.

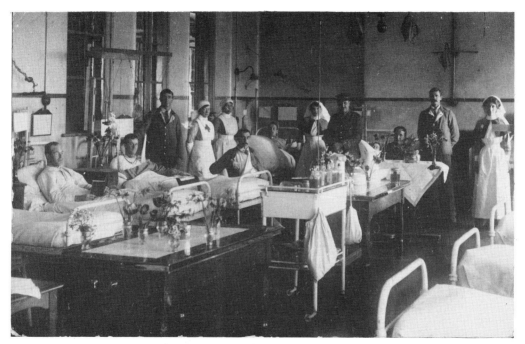

29A WARD, NETLEY, HAMPSHIRE, c. 1917
This was a hospital for the Royal Navy's wounded men. The VAD on the left of the picture, wearing a red cross on her apron, has completed her one year's training and next to her is a VAD in training. The message on the reverse of the postcard reads: "Dear Ma, photo of our staff and Dr who is a good clever Dr and has 150 cases to deal with, with love ".

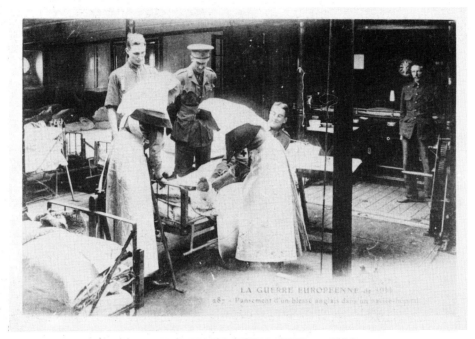

AN UNKNOWN HOSPITAL SHIP, c. 1916
This naval hospital is on board an unknown ship, with Q.A.s attending the wounded.
The Royal Navy specially commissioned some ships as hospital-ships. As can be seen,
this postcard was published in France.

A WARD IN 1ST EASTERN GENERAL HOSPITAL, CAMBRIDGE, c. 1918
Showing one of the many quickly-constructed timber huts for hospital use. Some of
these huts are still used as hospitals. Notice the flags of the Allies hanging from the
rafters, and the shortage of space.

OFF DUTY

ALICE, c. 1905
With very little money, cousin
Alice could not afford to go out.
She writes on this card to Mary
saying that she is sorry she
has not been up to see her
"but we only get off once every
14 days". This speaks for itself
and Alice does look very tired.
The postcard is not postmarked
so there is no indication as to
who she was or where she
worked.

NURSES' HOME, BEECHCROFT ROAD, ESSEX, c. 1910
What a noisy place this would have been - right next to a Day Nursery! A nurse had to be in each evening by !0.00 p.m. or else was "on the mat". However, in most nurses' homes there were ways of smuggling in late if you were careful, although it might have meant climbing in through the mortuary window! Notice the high walls with railings on top to defer late-comers.

THE LONDON "SET", 6th June 1917
It was not all work and no play. This is perhaps one of the happiest pictures in this book.
Drinking tea is always popular with nurses - how many cups of refreshing tea were
gulped down behind the kitchen door? If Sister or Matron caught you.....!
The London is the largest hospital in the East End (see page 18).

THE NURSES' SITTING ROOM, ST. GEORGE'S INFIRMARY, c. 1912
A nurse appears to be asleep on her afternoon off, even though the chair looks very
uncomfortable. The piano takes the place of today's television set. On this postcard,
Flo writes: "I am so tired in the morning. This is our sitting room...". Staff nurses usually
had a more pleasant sitting room and, further up the hierarchy, Sisters did even better.

"FOUR NURSES SITTING IN THE MORNING SUN AFTER NIGHT DUTY", c. 1913
The message reads: "What do you think of this? Don't look at my eyes too closely we
have been up all night. See the caramels (or the empty box), Love from Mary". The card
is postmarked Bristol but the hats are not those of Bristol Royal Infirmary.

NURSES' SITTING ROOM, UNKNOWN LOCATION, c. 1915
Two of the nurses are wearing their hospital badges which were given on completion of their three years' training and, often, a further year as a staff nurse. A home Sister was attached to each nurses' home and her job was to see that bedrooms were always left tidy with slippers off the floor and stored away. At one famous London hospital, if a nurse's bedroom clothes-drawers were untidy, she would have to miss her short coffee break to tidy up. The nurses appear to be engrossed in their own thoughts.

"TIME FOR TEA", KENDAL, c. 1907
Every picture tells a story - but what is this one? Is it a new probationer being given
the "once-over"? Does this young lady, wearing the large, brimmed hat typical of the
period, really know what she is letting herself in for?

THE LONG DAY CLOSES

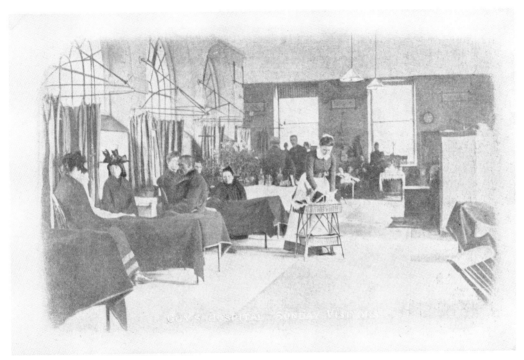

SUNDAY VISITORS, GUY'S HOSPITAL, c. 1900
When in hospital, a patient always looks forward to visitors but, in those days,
visiting was strictly limited. At the appointed time, a nurse would ring a bell to
announce the end of visiting. In the mid-Fifties, visiting cards had to be shown.
Too many visitors can certainly tire a patient and does no good at all. In this picture,
everyone looks very solemn indeed - but the hat, second from left, is enough to cheer
the proceedings!

Poplar and Stepney Sick Asylum, E.   The Cor.....

THE 1/4 MILE LONG CORRIDOR, POPLAR AND STEPNEY SICK ASYLUM, c. 1912
At the end of the long hospital day, the corridors and floors were washed. This hospital
was founded "for the reception of the pauper sick", under the provisions of the Poor Act,
1867. Many large hospitals have long corridors for the staff to walk - before even getting
to the patients. With corridors like this one, how long would it take a
nurse to walk to the dining room for her short 20-minute coffee break?

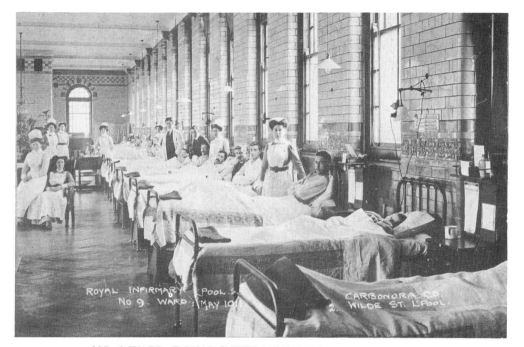

NO. 9 WARD, ROYAL INFIRMARY, LIVERPOOL, May 1911
The day staff have made their patients comfortable, the charts are in order, the sluices clean and tidy - all is ready for the night staff to take over. The hospital never closes - how can it? Sister would take the night nurse around the ward, passing each patient's bed and giving her report.
This beautiful old Infirmary, founded in 1749, has been empty now for ten years. Notice the brass plaque over the bed on the right.

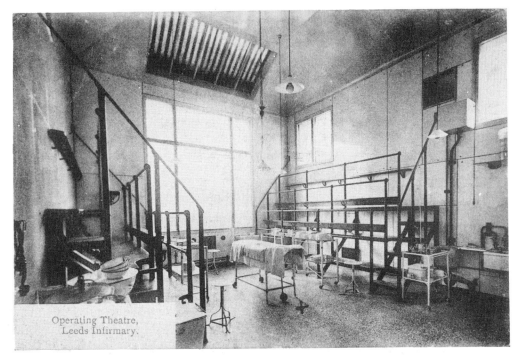

Operating Theatre,
Leeds Infirmary.

THE OPERATING THEATRE, LEEDS INFIRMARY, c. 1902
The theatre is empty at last! The message reads: "Dear Mother, I thought you would like
this view as this is where I stood. The gallery is where the surgeons stand at an
important operation. My feet are not quite so bad just now, hope they will get right
soon. Love to all, Gerty".
She stood at the head of the table - where the cross is on this postcard. On Ward 10 of
this Infirmary, an aspidistra plant is said to have lived for 80 years but, sadly, it died
when Sister moved from the ward. The aspidistra did not like the move and just had to
show its resentment!

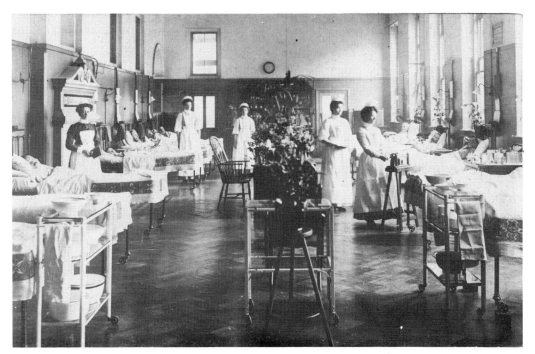

KING'S COLLEGE HOSPITAL, LONDON, c. 1900
One of the famous London teaching hospitals, it was founded in 1839 and moved to new
buildings in Denmark Hill in 1913. Its medical school was founded in 1831 and was
affiliated to London University in 1909. Notice the bandage-rolling machine on the right
of the picture - an article now long disposed of. The trolley is laid up ready for the next
blanket bath.

**A STAFF NURSE,
BATH EYE INFIRMARY,**
c. 1910
When they come on night duty,
the night staff will check the
wards and equipment. Here,
Staff Nurse has carefully
checked her trolley and seen
that all is in correct working
order and ready for any
emergency. Today, there are
24 different eye hospitals in
Great Britain. How our ancestors
of the Bath Eye Infirmary would
have marvelled at the eye
surgery of today.

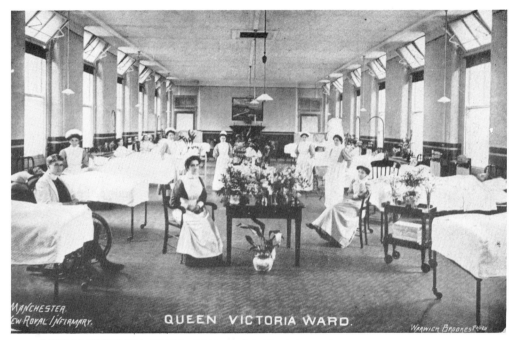

QUEEN VICTORIA WARD, MANCHESTER NEW ROYAL INFIRMARY, c. 1912
At last, time for a sit down - never! A nurse was only allowed to sit down to feed a
patient or, on night duty, when the ward was quiet, her fingers were kept busy making
cotton-wool balls and dressings. The doctor appears to be sitting in a wheelchair. Notice
Sister in her dark dress and her aspidistra plant on the floor. The first Manchester
Infirmary was built in 1752, now known as Manchester New Royal having 663 beds.

THE CLOCK TOWER AND INFIRMARY, SALISBURY, c. 1904

The visitors have all left as the last horse and carriage draws away. Crickets begin to chirp in the boiler room; the ward is quiet. Be it the famous "Jimmy's" of the television series, your local hospital or small cottage hospital, the wonderful uninterrupted tradition of service continues. "Nurse please", calls a frail voice.

Chimes from the clock herald the long night.

"Bless all those who serve the sick in body or mind. God grant us a peaceful night. Let us remember our benefactors both living and dead, Amen".

INDEX

INDEX CONTINUED